Majnūn Leyla:

Poems about Passion

Joyce Åkesson

Pallas Athena

Lund

2009

CONTENT

Majnün Leyla:
Poems about Passion

*"Let the lover be disgraceful, crazy,
Absentminded. Someone sober
Will worry about things going badly.
Let the lover be."*

Rumi.

Preface

I have been interested in Arabic poetry for many years. Many of the old Classical Arabic verses have already found their way into my book *Arabic Morphology and Phonology* and into my other Arabic linguistic works as well. A few verses from the 7ᵗʰ century written by Majnūn al-ᶜĀmirī were also included among them.[1] In 1994, I have also written an article about this poet that has been published in a literary magazine in Sweden.[2]

Majnūn's poems express an incurable romanticism, the deepest longings of the heart for its beloved, nostalgia, memories of a lost paradise, idealism, anticipation, joy after a reunion, bitterness after a separation, lovesickness, wandering in the desert and a consuming passion. The beloved, Leyla, is elevated and appears superior to everyone. Although Majnūn is a faithful Muslim who performs pilgrimage, he is most faithful to Leyla.

It is interesting to remark that the romantic love poetry has developed in Arabia around the 7ᵗʰ century before that it was pursued in Europe by the troubadours of southern France in the 13th and 14th centuries.

Majnūn's poems are known to belong to the genre of the *ash°ār al-ghazal al-udhri* "platonic or virginal love poems", which emphasize on the spiritual love[3] as opposed to *ash°ār al-ghazal* "erotic poems",[4] which emphasize on the woman's physical beauty and on the desire that it arouses in her lover.

There are about 325 Arabic poems by Majnūn al-°Āmirī that are presented and commented on in the *Dīwān majnūn Leyla* by Farrāj.

I have chosen 62 poems among them that I have interpreted and set in the free verse of English poetry.

Beside studying the poems in the *Dīwān* I have also had the privilege to read André Miquel's translation of several poems into French in his book, *Majnūn, L'amour poème.*

The Classical Arabic poems are known for using a complicated play with words that can have double meanings or different ambiguous meanings. The verses are rhymed and measured and follow one of the sixteen different established meters. The meters are known as *buḥūr* "seas", and each unit of the seas is known as *taf°īla*. As there is a certain number of *taf°īlas* in every sea, the measuring procedure of a poem is very rigorous, and sometimes only the fact of adding or removing a consonant or a vowel can shift the verse from one meter to another. Also every verse has to end with the same rhyme throughout the poem. These complexities may in themselves explain how impossible it is to get the same rhythm in the

English translation. A literal translation of the poems is hence impossible as there are words and expressions that are acceptable in a language and heavy and unacceptable in another.

I have in most cases indicated in my notes the poem's meter and the last rhyme. In the case of a changeable consonant I have used the sign &. In order to explain the contents of a specific poem I have in some cases introduced its background. I have referred in the notes to the different works from which each poem is selected and I have commented on a few issues whenever I felt that this was necessary. It is my hope that this book presents an English interpretation of Majnun's love poems and that it can offer to the reader a feeling of the poems' contents and structures.

I would like to extend my heartfelt appreciation to my friends and family for being there. In particular, I thank very much my mother, Irene Egeland, for her encouragement and support. I am also very grateful to my husband, Anders, for his insightful comments and stimulating ideas and to our son, Filip, for his interest and enthusiasm.

Introduction

Majnūn al-ᶜĀmirī

Majnūn al-ᶜĀmirī "The Madman from the tribe of Banū ᶜĀmir" was also known as Majnūn Leyla "the one who was obsessed or mad about Leyla". His real name was Qays b. al-Mulawwaḥ.[5] He was from the Banū ᶜĀmir tribe in the northern Arabian Peninsula and lived during the Ummayad era in the 7th century.

The early stories and poems about him were documented in at least three influential collections, namely: 1) the *Basṭ ṣāmiᶜ al-Masāmir* by Muḥammad b. ᶜAlī b. Maḥmūd b. Ṭūlūn (d. 953), 2) the encyclopedic collection of over 20 volumes, the *Kitāb al-Aghānī "The Book of Songs"*[6] by the Arab litterateur of Qurayshī origin, Abu'l-Faraj al-Aṣfahānī (d. 967) and 3) the *Maṣāriᶜ al-ᶜushshāq* by Jaᶜfar b. Aḥmad al-Sarrāj (d. 1106).

Some scholars however doubt of Majnūn's existence and believe that his character was created in order to illustrate the ideal lover. A source tells:

"Al-Aṣmaᶜī said: "I asked an Arab from the Banū ᶜĀmir b. Ṣaᶜṣaᶜ tribe about Majnūn al-ᶜĀmirī and he answered: "Who are you asking me about? Many among us have become mad because of love."

I then said: "About the one who loved Leyla."

"They all loved Leyla," he said."[7]

This source indicates that different poets from this early period could have written these passionate Arabic poems to a woman named Leyla, and that their poetry has wrongly been attributed to Majnūn. This is perhaps not very strange as there are many lovers among the Arabs, and that many among these lovers pertained to the Banū ᶜĀmir tribe, and that there were many Arabic women who were named Leyla.[8]

According to Al-Jāḥiẓ, it has become very common that many persons used to refer to Majnūn every time that they read a love poem by an anonymous poet written to a certain woman named Leyla.[9]

The story of Majnūn and Leyla on which the poems are based

Whether Majnūn existed or whether he was a fictive character is an issue that can be debated. Many believe however that he existed and that he is the sole author of these passionate love poems.

What is certain is that the story of Leyla and Majnūn exists and that it is famous in the Islamic world. It is a tragic story of endless love, much like the later stories of *Tristan and Isolde* and *Romeo and Juliet* in Europe. It has spread and has been told in legends, songs, poems, plays and epics extending from the Caucasus to Africa and from the Atlantic to the Indian Ocean.

It tells about Qays b. al-Mulawwaḥ who fell in love with his cousin Leylā bint Mahdīy (d. 688), better known as Leyla al-ᶜĀmirīya.[10] They were both from the same tribe and used to spend a lot of time together, tending their parents' flocks in a mountain called al-Tawbād. Leyla returned Qays' love quietly while Qays became so obsessively in love with her that he started writing romantic passionate poems about her. When Qays' poetry became very famous and the people started to discuss them and recite them, Leyla's parents became very annoyed about all the noise they caused around her and decided to marry her to Ward b. Muḥammad in order to save her reputation. It is then that Qays became desperate and known as Majnūn Leyla "driven mad by Leyla". His family tried to marry him with other women, but he refused to marry.

His faithfulness to Leyla is illustrated by this story:

"Some women from his tribe sat with him and said:

"Why have you isolated yourself? What do you see in Leyla when she is just a woman among many other women? Is it not better that you love one of us so that we can reciprocate your feelings and you can get your reason back and your body will heal?"

He then answered: "If I was able to transfer the love that I have for her to you, I would have done so, and then I would have taken away my love from everyone after her and I would have lived among the people in peace."

And they told him: "What is it that infatuated you in her?"

He said: "Everything that I have seen, contemplated and heard has infatuated me. By God, I haven't seen anything at all in her unless that it was beautiful in my eyes. And I have tried hard to find something in her that was ugly or disgraceful in order to forget her, but I did not find anything."[11]

Before that Leyla married she visited Qays once and tried to cheer him up, which is illustrated by this story:

"When Majnūn became more desperate, his mother visited Leyla and said to her: "Qays has become so madly in love with you and he neither eats and drinks anymore. Perhaps that you should visit him for a little while so that he gets his senses back."

Leyla said: "At day I cannot come… but at night."

And she came at night and said to him: "Oh Qays, your mother states that you have become mad because of me and that you neither eat or drink. Pray to God for his mercy and control yourself!"

So he cried… and she cried with him, and they talked together until dawn. Then she bade farewell and left him."[12]

Qays' family tried to make Leyla's father change his mind and marry his daughter off with him, but without any success. Leyla's father was stubborn and considered that Qays has destroyed his daughter's reputation with his poems and that he must defend her honor before the whole tribe. Qays would never be allowed to marry Leyla and Leyla shall marry Ward.

Qays' father took him then to Mecca so that he becomes cured from his passion, but this didn't help him, as this story tells:

"When they were wandering in the Ka°ba, his father said to him: "… Pray to God that He frees you from your love to Leyla."

… But then Majnūn said: "Oh God, do so that my love for Leyla always grows,,, and do not ever let me forget her!"[13]

It is not so strange that such a passion awakens the jealous spirit. Majnūn and Leyla's husband did not have the warmest feelings for each other. The following episode illustrates this:

"When they returned from Mecca, Majnūn happened to run into Leyla's husband... and he asked him:

> *"By Your God, have you embraced Leyla*
> *before dawn or kissed her mouth?*
> *and has Leyla's radiance revealed itself to you*
> *like the damp daisy in its radiance? "*

Ward replied: "If you want me to swear by God, yes, I've done so." And he recited:

> *"I have embraced her and kissed her cheek*
> *like a rose with a reviving scent,*
> *and I have bent over her mouth*
> *and drank from a wine*
> *with which I could calm the worries in my heart."*

So Majnun took two pieces of burning coal in his hands that he squeezed until he fainted."[14]

The love between Majnūn and Leyla was not only platonic in spite of the fact that she is described as pure. A source tells:

"Once when Leyla's husband and her father traveled to Mecca, Leyla sent a servant to Majnūn, inviting him to visit her. She said to him: "Come to me every night as long as the people are away."

He was then able to pass the time with her until they came back."[15]

Leyla moved to Iraq with her husband, where she became ill and eventually died. Upon hearing the news of her death, Qays emerged from the wilderness to visit her grave. He was later found dead in 688 A.D. near it. He had carved three verses of poetry on a rock near the grave, and they were the last three verses attributed to him.

Leyla al-ᶜĀmirīya

According to the story, Leyla was very beautiful and loved Qays as much as he loved her. A source tells:

"A man took a journey toward Damascus and al-Ḥijāz and then Taymāᵓ, al-Surāt and Najd... When he found himself in a tent that was set up for him because it was raining... a woman asked him from where he was coming. The man answered: "From Tahāma and the surroundings of Najd.""

So I went in to a corner of the tent and she hanged up a curtain between us. Then she said to me: "Oh God's servant, which parts of Najd have you passed by?"

I answered: "The whole of Najd".

She said: "By whom have you lived there?"

I said: "By the Banū ᶜĀmir."

She then sighed deeply and said: "By which Banū ᶜĀmir have you been?"

I said: "By the Banū Ḥuraysh."

She then started to cry and said: "Did you hear anyone talking about a young man whose name is Qays b. al-Mulawwaḥ and whom they call Majnūn?"

I said: "Of course, by God, I have lived at his father's place and I have seen him wandering in the desert, living with the wild animals and not gaining back his consciousness until someone mentioned for him a woman whose name is Leyla. He then cried and recited poems about her..."

She then lifted the curtain that hanged between me and her, and I could see a woman beautiful as the moon, - of the kind of beauty that I have never seen before -, and she cried until I thought that her heart would break. And I said: "Oh woman, call God for help. Have I said anything disturbing?"

But she remained a long time in this state of sorrow and tears... until she fainted. Then I asked her: "Who are you, Oh God's servant, and what is your life's story?"

She answered: "I am Leyla who has given him a lot of unhappiness and whom he could never have."

And I have never seen such a sorrow and passion that resembled hers."[16]

This story reveals that she loved Qays as much as he loved her.

Before her marriage, Leyla had also promised to be faithful to him. A tradition tells the words she said to Majnūn after that he revealed his love to her:

"I swear by God that I shall never, as long as I live, be together with any other man than you, unless if I am forced to it."

The following verses, which are written by Leyla reveal her love:

"Majnūn would not have been in this state
if I hadn't been in the same state as well,
but I have concealed my love
while he has declaimed his."[17]

The spread of the Arabic story

The Arabic story of Majnūn and Leyla spread and passed into the Persian literature. The lovers were mentioned by the Persian poet, Abu Abdullah Jafar b. Mohammad ibn Hakim b. Abdurrahman b. Adam Rudaki Samarghandi, known also as Rudagi or Rudhagi, (d. 941), but it is mostly the romantic epic poet Nizām al-Dīn Abū Muḥammad Ilyās b. Yūsuf b. Zakī b. Mu'ayyad (d. 1209), known as Nezami Ganjavi, who popularized it dramatically in his masterpiece.[18] Nezami collected both secular and mystical sources about Majnūn and portrayed a vivid picture of the famous lovers. Numerous translations of Nezami's work appeared in many languages encompassed by the Islamic religious culture.

It is believed that at least forty Persian and thirteen Turkish versions exist. Among the Persian poets who imitated Nezami and who wrote their own versions of the story, Saᶜd al-Shīrāzī (d. 1291), Amīr Khasrū al-Dahlawī (d. 1325), ᶜAbd al-Raḥmān al-Jāmī (d. 1492) and ᶜAbdallah Hātifī (d. 1521) can be mentioned.

The Persianized work, - which should not be confused with the poems that are interpreted here, - also passed into the English language in the eighteenth century indirectly, based on a few translations of an imitation of Nezami's romance. Sir William Jones (1746-94) introduced Nezami to the English world in several of his publications. He did not translate any of Nezami's romances, but did publish a Persian edition of Hātifī 's (d. 1520) *Leyli o Majnun* in 1788. This version of the romance became a source of inspiration for Isaac D'Israeli (1766-1848), who made an adaptation in English. D'Israeli's work was later put into the opera *Kais, or Love in the Deserts: An Opera in Four Acts* by William Reeve, which was performed in London at the Theatre Royal in Drury Lane.

Louis Aragon (1897-1982), one of the leading representatives of the Surrealist movement, bemoaned his love for his beloved in *Le Fou d'Elsa* (1963). Aragon's version was based on Jāmi's *Leyli and Majnun*, which again is an imitation of Nezami's version. The first translation of the romance was an abridged verse rendition by James Atkinson published in 1836, which was used by Eric Clapton in the late 1970s for certain lyrics on his recording of *Leyla and Other Love Songs*. It has been reprinted several times (1894, 1915). In recent decades, several translations, adaptations and performances of this romance have appeared in English, of which those by Rudolf Gelpke (originally in German) in collaboration with E. Mattin and G. Hill.

The famous Egyptian writer Aḥmad Shawqī (1868-1932) has also dramatized the story for the theatre. His poetic play is now considered one of the best in modern Arab poetry. Qays' lines from the play are sometimes confused with his actual poems.

The story was also adapted in the Azerbaijani language in the 16th century by Fuzūlī. The Azerbajani famous composer

Uzeyir Hajibeyov used the material to create what became the Middle East's first opera. It premiered in Baku in 1908.

The legend had become so famous that in India it is believed that Laila and Majnu found refuge in a village in Rajasthan before dying. The graves of Laila and Majnu are believed to be located in the Bijnore village near Anupgarth in the Sringanganagar district. According to a rural legend there, Laila and Majnun were from Sindh and escaped to these parts and died there. Hundreds of newly weds and lovers from India and Pakistan still attend the two-day fair in June.

There is also a Laila-Majnun tomb in Al-Hofuf in Saudi Arabia.

Majnūn and mysticism

Many Sūfī mystics considered Majnūn's love for Leyla as the soul's search for an absolute union with God. They also told many stories about Majnūn in order to illustrate a few mystical concepts such as annihilation, love-madness, self-sacrifice, etc.

Majnun's selfless love and the way he had lost himself in the beloved were particularly attractive to them. Majnun provided mystics with a palpable example of 'annihilation' in the Beloved.

Jalaluddin Rumi writes in his *Mathnawi:*

"The beloved is all in all, the lover only veils him.
The beloved is all that lives, the lover a dead thing."

And furthermore, he writes:

"God made Majnun love Leyla so much that
Just her dog would cause confusion in him.

There are thousands of wines that can take over our
minds.
Don't think all ecstasies are the same!"[19]

In his discourse on "True Discipleship", Meher Baba, the Indian mystic and spiritual master who declared publicly in 1954 that he was the Avatar of the age, uses the story of Majnūn and Leyla as an example about how all love leads to the Master:

"The fundamental requisite for the candidate who would be a true disciple is an unquestioning love for the Master. All the other streams of love ultimately join this great river and disappear in it; this is illustrated by the story of Majnun and Leyla. Majnun loved Leyla so intensely that every moment of his life he was filled with thoughts about her. The utter self-denial and sincerity of his love ultimately led him to his master."

The Poems

(1)

They told me: "If you want
you can forget her!"

But I said: "I do not want and I cannot
because my love for her is tied to my heart
like the well bucket to the cord!
Of this endless love my soul knows the power!

But they mock me,
they scold me
and they drive me away
because they know
that their slanders destroy me![1]

(2)

Majnūn met a man who was coming from Najd. He started questioning him about Leyla and Najd. After that, he recited these verses while he was crying.

O Najd's wonders!

Oh, how fragrant is Najd's earth

and its people

if Najd is still the same!

When can I praise Qanā's two mountains?

I have been for too long separated from them,

I do not dare more to believe

that everything is still the same!

I think of you too when the evening falls,

you, daisy of the sands,

damp from the soft dew of dawn,

how did you endure the night?

And you, young women,

have you moved somewhere else

or are you still living there

between al-Batīl[2] and al-Ḥimā?

I think of the wind

that smells lavender

and that is blowing there.

Will it pass by Najd?

Oh may I feel it again playing

in my free and wild hair,

when I am riding a horse

with thin sides that is speeding!

May I be able to hear

in the green meadows

from valley to valley,

our camels groan![3]

(3)

My love for you, Oh Leyla,

has made me famous,

and the whole world has heard

about the misery I am going through.

Suffocated by a cruel passion,

abandoned to despair,

I suffer.

Who can rescue me?

Leyla, Oh my longing!

Oh you whose gaze

has ignited this tormenting fire in my heart!

Do not hate me

because I'll die if you drive me away!

Are you Leyla?

Then be considerate and tender.

I am your prisoner,

I love you,

by God, believe me!

My soul is revived by this love that I conceal

from fear of a slanderer or an envious spy,

who would reveal to the people

everything they did not know.[4]

(4)

Oh you morning bird,
fly away and carry my greeting to her.

Let me hope when I call out.
May God lead you forward to her!

If you return to the earth,
let it be to Leyla's country,
- a desert in which one gets lost,
but which ties my soul
and heart in its knot -.

Oh! I dream of a day
when nothing separates us.
I live of that dream,
it is my final hope![5]

(5)

I only want to travel

if the road takes me northward,

and I only like the lightning

if it strikes in Yemen!

For a woman like Leyla

any man would want to kill himself,

even if like me,

he could accustom himself to despair.

If it is important to dream about peace and serenity,

then I want, Oh Leyla, to meet you all alone.

Weakness has taken its hold of my body

and a sadness subsists

from the morning until the evening.

Love's messenger calls:

"Where is the prisoner?

He persists always,

and always more and more!"

Oh! Much shall my heart endure

if it goes on loving.

Hold your breath, Oh death,

for love is my pledge![6]

(6)

They forbade me to visit her

on the day that she traveled,

but my crying eyes

bade her farewell.

They forbade me to talk to her.

Oh, who has seen a lover in tears,

a heart that bids farewell?

"Oh, may you have God's protection

and my greeting,

right from the time that the sun rises

until it sets!"[7]

(7)

If she looked my way

her eyes talked to me,

and then my eyes answered her back silently.

"We shall meet again".

Her eyes predict it,

but then in the same eyes

it is death that is waiting for me.

I fear, I despair,

I die and I live again through my hope.

How many times have I not been dead

and resuscitated?

They are all here around me,

men, *jinns,*

but I do not care!

If they think they can forbid me from seeing you:

I shall come to you anyway![8]

(8)

She gave me a sign with her eyes

of fear for her parents,

- a sad sign,

which did not need any words -.

But I understood that her look

was telling me hello

and welcoming my entranced soul.[9]

(9)

The good persons
are only those who can love.

Nothing positive
can be created by someone
who neither can love
or be in love.

If I am reproachful to her,
she says: "I swear by your life,
I do not wish anything more
than that we reunite and never separate.

If you long for me,
then come to my door.
for I long for you
even more."[10]

(10)

Your whole body in its garment

is radiant in its beauty and gaiety, Oh Leyla.

Oh! How I wish that I could be revived

by its refreshing warmth!

I have seen you,

I have seen you,

- was it in my dreams -?

or with my loving eyes

in the light of the day?

I said holding you in my arms:

"My fire dies!"

But no, the fire does not die.

It still burns,

it is stronger![11]

(11)

When the night falls and the dawn breaks,

I dream of a pure and beautiful virgin,

slender and tender, with nice curves,

thin waist and round breasts,

moving steadily like a mare

on a muddy soil.

Her neck is the neck of the desert deer.

Her eyes remind of the buffalo's big eyes.

Her lower third part is strong as iron,

glittering as a river.

Her middle third part is a sand dune.

Her upper third part are branches and bunches of grapes,

fragrant and filled with sweet juices.

Her eyes aim right and hit all the men's hearts:

no one can avoid their deadly arrows.

She has sown the seeds of love in my heart
and watered them with the water of longing
that sleeps in her big eyes.

This terrified heart,
you know well how to hit it,
Oh you the gracious and languishing arrow,
embellished by feathers and make-up.

Truly, the beautiful woman
can make her lover's blood shed
without feeling any remorse
or paying a price.

By God, she could kill violently
the one who loves her
without fearing the law
or the hand of justice,

for when did justice intervene
in the matters of love?[12]

(12)

Her beauty is like wine,
her saliva and its clarity too.

Three kinds of wine
have mixed together in her,
one more intoxicating than the other.[13]

(13)

Oh the worst of misery!

Our farewell day.

"I know," she said,

"who I shall leave in the hands of God."

But can I now in my loneliness

silence my soul

when my loving heart

is not able to repress this love any more?

Oh God, my God,

my Almighty God,

my life leaves me,

she goes her way,

I cannot stop her.

When I disappear, my friends,

go to where I sleep,

and then say to Leyla:

"You have left him,

he is dead."[14]

(14)

I love you, Oh my Leyla,

I persist on loving you,

you, who near or far,

think only of avoiding me!

I love you, Oh my Leyla,

and the smallest sigh of this love,

carried away by the wind, inhaled,

would trigger a deep torment

in a passerby's soul.

Yes, I complain to her

about this longing,

in public and all alone.

All silently I tell her

about my heart's sorrow.

If I beg for her help,

she is deaf for my prayers,

then I pray to God.

What do I gain if I see her close to me?

Tears.

In love and entranced,

so terrible it is if she is near![15]

(15)

When I saw the mountain of Tawbād,

my heart was seized by sorrow.

When it saw me

it invoked the Merciful.

When I recognized it

I started immediately to cry.

It called me with its highest voice.

"In your surroundings", I said, "I had friends.

It was the bright time, the happy one, the past."

"They are all gone", it said.

"It is now I who am guarding their land.

Who can resist Destiny?

Everything changes,

but you know that well."

Today I cry, and tomorrow?

I feel terrified.

Our tribes are now united,

but you shall also go your way.

Oh this water that richly flows out of its bowl,

heavy showers, storms, silent rains,

Oh tears![16]

(16)

Is it the camp's fault

that it is situated in the Orient

or a sand dune's

that an eastern or southern wind erases?

These horses,

Oh! I wish they were dead!

They can so well separate the lovers!

Trotting away since dawn

and always faithful to a meeting;

my heart's dearest part has left me

without leaving a trace![17]

(17)

When I pass by the house,

Leyla's house,

I kiss its walls,

this one and that one.

"Is it of loving the walls

that you have lost your senses?"

"No, not the walls, my friend,

but the one who lives behind the walls!"[18]

(18)

Majnūn came to visit Leyla in the camp, but did not find her
anywhere. He then started to kiss the earth.

I kiss the earth

on which your foot has stepped,

Oh soft Leyla.

They say: "Look at the madman.

See what he is doing!"

Do I love the earth so much

that I have to kiss it?

No! It is you that I love

and your steps on it.

It is you whom I am madly in love with.

It is because of you that I find comfort

in the memories that torment me.

For ever separated from the towns,

in the desert I must live,

hoping there to find some peace

among the beasts![19]

(19)

Must they hit Leyla every time
that I visit her dwelling?

Is it the lamb's fault
that the wolf is drawn to this enclosure!

The one who honors Leyla honors me,
the one who despises her despises me,
for truly, Leyla is my soul's happiness and goodness.

It is of no use to forbid Leyla to greet me,
to lock her in and to continuously spy on her,
as I shall not give her up
even if I must defy the brandished swords,
and I shall look for her in the whole camp
until I find her!

Alas! If the happy destiny

that I wish for Leyla, was mine!

Oh! May she never experience

the sad destiny that she has chosen for me!

Oh! Do not blame me if I put my life at risk:

The place of every soul is by its beloved.[20]

(20)

They asked me once when I came to visit their quarter

with a fire in my heart that was burning:

"Are you not afraid of our lions?"

And I answered:

"The place of every soul is by its beloved"![21]

(21)

When Majnūn went to visit Leyla, her family forbade her to receive him. He cried then and recited these verses:

Both of us know, Oh Leyla,

that you have cried of compassion

and love over me.

Is it not strange that we both live in a country

in which we cannot more see each other

and in which we are in agony?

I have been afflicted by infatuation,

love and glowing passion.

You are probably mourning over an orphaned slave,

because a woman like you, Oh Leyla,

is compassionate and tender.

Reason, Oh Leyla,

has cried bitter tears over me,

when it knew about the hardships

that my heart was enduring.[22]

(22)

I honor you and fear you.

Shall I defy your power?

No, you are the apple of my eye!

Shall I abandon you?

No, You live in my soul,

Leyla, you who gave me so little happiness!

Oh the kindest of people

who say every time they see me coming:

"Here comes Leyla's beloved!"

Shall they hit Leyla

every time that I pass by her dwelling?

Spare the innocent

when the wolf is drawn to this enclosure![23]

(23)

You shall greet, Oh sun,

Leyla and her family.

But when? Tell me:

at dawn or when you set?

Why do they hit Leyla every time

when I pass by her dwelling?

It is not Leyla's fault

if the wolf is drawn to the enclosure.

But if your anger must be stilled,

stone me to death the day when I say:

"The wolf has gone away

with his sense of smell

and his cutting teeth!"[24]

(24)

Oh the remains of the camp,

Oh the soft presence,

for the wandering wild man

when the evening falls!

When his heart sees them

it becomes filled with hope.

I honor you and fear you.

Shall I defy your power?

No. You are the apple of my eye![25]

(25)

When Majnūn was asleep, a man woke him up and told him:

"Leyla is in Iraq and is sick,
how can you be lying down like this,
unaffected and asleep?"

He then fainted, and when he awoke he recited these verses.

They say: "Leyla is in Iraq and is sick

How can you, who are her friend,

be so unaffected?"

May God cure all the sick people in Iraq,

because I feel sorry for all the sick people there!

If it is true that Leya is in Iraq and is sick

than the sea of death can hold me in its arms

and drown me!

Lost, I wander from place to place

and the morning closes again the path to Leyla,

Someone, I think, has lit a flame in my heart
which has spread and burst into bolts of lightning!

With bitter tears and with a last wheeze,
my soul remembers you
and dies of love.

I have delighted in a sun,
which pulls the full moon to its shame,
and which conceals the lightning when it strikes.

Blacker than pitch are your locks
and clearer than the moon is your face.
Oh grace! Of perfect beauty!

I have become madly in love and restless,
and I am suffering like a slave in chains!

My reason has weakened

and sleep has left me.

All this is too unbearable for a heart
which pounds hard and cries.

Nothing more remains of me
than bones and veins:
my love for her has destroyed my body,
my heart and my soul.

If I die, do not blame me,
but pity me:
a lost soul deserves
that one cries over it.

Then write these words
over my gravestone:
"It was eyes that killed him.
He is dead as a lover."

To God I complain

and ask for His Mercy.

I have loved and endured too much!
My heart continues to burn for Leyla.[26]

(26)

I say to my friends: "She is the sun.

Its light surrounds you

but it remains distant

and inaccessible to everyone!"

But the wind hit me right in the heart:

It was her breath.

Oh scent! Oh freshness!

The end comes now.

Unconscious and impatient,

all the words have left me.

They carry me,

they take me away,

I hear my relatives cry,

wanting to sacrifice their lives

if they only could rescue me! [27]

(27)

When Majnūn was wandering around, he met a few shepherds who told him that Leyla's parents have taken her away to meet the man whom they chose for her to marry.

Oh night's shepherds,

see how the morning's first soft hours

have weakened me!

Oh! What are they doing,

those who have captivated my heart?

Have they pitched their camp somewhere,

or when the night has fallen,

have they moved away?

And why are these stars

always hanging

in the lovers' hearts?

"Tomorrow Leyla al-ᶜĀmirīya[28]

shall go away

or maybe even tonight".

Oh these words in the night,

poor heart,

defeated heart,

like the grey partridge

in the net!

Courageously she fights,

but her wings are for ever caught.

Her chicks are in the desert,

defenseless and abandoned.

The wind blows angrily

and overturns their nest.

When they hear it howling,

they shiver and call:

"Oh mother, it is time!

The evening is here. Return!"

But this hope disappears in the night,
there is no use,
and no help either comes in the morning.

Oh night's shepherds
live as you please.
I was already dead
when I could have loved![29]

(28)

You treat me so badly,

Oh soft breeze,

you who in the happy days

could bring me so much comfort!

If ever there is a man,

one only man in the whole world,

who is weary of love,

Oh breeze, it is I.

And if a deadly poison

mixed with her saliva, [30]

one only sip would suffice

to quench my thirst![31]

(29)

Do not suffer, Oh loving heart,

but rather die quickly filled with sorrow.

Our torments in this world

always have an end.

You love a woman

whom only Eternity can give you.

Go, strive,

try to find a path

to the one who, day after day,

must here avoid you.

You love a woman

whose face resembles a deer's,

and whose beauty, like the sun's,

draws to it men's adoring eyes.

Your soul is burning,

and your heart is tormented,

and of love for her

your tears have become incessant.

Yes, your crying is the best witness

of the true love that you feel

for such a soft and pure maiden.

If only the happy days

could return!

But Alas! Who has ever seen them returning?

Come! Find consolation,

be strong,

as time does not kill

but strengthen your love.

Shall I ever see Leyla again?

She is far, so far away!

The words of the envious
have poisoned her soul.

How much longer shall you suffer,
Oh tormented heart?

To God I complain
about all these hardships,
and beg for His Mercy![32]

(30)

Help me, Oh my God,

I think of her all the time!

Leyla! What crime have I committed?

I am completely confused!

Why have you abandoned me?

My God! I do not know!

And what have I done to you?

Leyla, tell me about it!

Shall we not meet any more?

Death is then milder!

Shall I empty the glass

from which no one drinks?

Or shall I flee far away,

farther away,

without anyone by my side?

Or what shall I do?

Shall I reveal this secret?

Then I shall be lost.

Leyla is confused in her relation to me:

a man whom one avoids,

a man whom one slanders.

But if after our death

our souls would unite?

The earth's surface can in vain heighten[33]

to hide our coffins from each other,

my soul, outside of my decomposed bones,

shall like a bird fly to meet your soul.[34]

Yes, my uninhibited soul, Oh Leyla,

shall celebrate and rejoice

when it shall listen to your voice![35]

And I shall say to my eyes: "Cry,

cry endlessly!

Shed tears or blod!"[36]

(31)

I die if she goes away,
I live if she comes near.

The eastern wind
revives my heart's torments.

And my eyes for Leyla
can only cry.

She lives in this soul
devoured by worries.

One hand, I believe,
holds my heart captive,
under nails covered with blood,
penetrating and hurting.[37]

(32)

I swear by Him

Who chose to live

over the Thabīr mountain[38]

where the clouds gather together!

By the tired and haggard camel,

which angrily speeds

through the dry desert!

That Leyla, since a long time

I love her,

she is my life

or my death.

- Other lovers can tell lies -.[39]

(33)

Love, I see it well,

is a glowing fire,

and of the lovers' hearts

it nourishes itself.

If only when they were burnt

they could finally die!

But alas! As soon as they have turned to ashes

they resuscitate, like the damned:[40]

their transformed skin,

again and again, restores itself

for new torments.[41]

(34)

She whom I ought to forget,
lives in my soul.
Whether I am glad or sad,
she occupies all my thoughts.

The evil people destroy her
with their slanders about me.
She fears them all
and drives me away,
except from her heart.

My country's wide horizons
have become narrow;
I have no friend
in whom I can delight in,
it is all Leylas fault.

For her sake I have loved

those who did not love me

and broken the ties

with those who did.

The loved one, the camp:

here is love,

here are the enemies.

Will you flee?

Will you visit her?

How shall I free myself

from love's hidden torments

when they have become my heart's joys

and its only choice?

The time of falling in love has died

before I have awaken,

but if I must die,

the mature love dies at the same time.

I have hidden my heart in vain

behind a veil,

my passion for you has torn the veil

and seized the heart.

My honor complains

over such a demanding love,

but you are the gift

or the enemy to fear.[42]

(35)

To Leyla's country
passion takes me.
I want to reproach her
the love that tortures me.

My eyelids are clouds,
which pour down their rain upon the earth,
and my heart is devoured
by worries and pains.

I reveal to the camp
my excessive sorrow,
and like streams
my tears flow without restraint.

I draw you in the sand,
I talk to your picture,
Is it possible that the earth hears my prayers?

I imagine myself being close to you,

But alas! This speech and my pain's cry

go only to the earth.

No one says anything;

it is completely silent around me.

The one to whom I complain

remains mute.

My tears, when I have lost my hope,

fall down like the rain out of the clouds.

Mad about you and because of you,

I am the madman, I know,

and my heart of loving you

only suffers and burns.[43]

(36)

Oh you who are persecuting me,

learn something about my life,

how in the desert

I spend my days.

I have tamed the grey partridge,

and the desert's wild animals

are grazing around me.

I swear by your life,

what can I do better, every day,

than to draw you in the sand,

and rejoice about the language of the stones?[44]

I have also gained the wild animals' friendship.

Wild? Not for me,

whether they are males, females,

first-borns or suckles.

I shall not talk about the cruel loneliness,

about my life in the desert,

about my passion for her;

Oh gathered pains that keep on haunting me![45]

(37)

If you send her my greeting, Oh friend,

she will, devastated by sorrow,

break out into tears,

and the concealed love in her troubled heart

will reveal itself by one only word from me.

And against her will she will then cry rivers,

and nothing in the world will gladden her any more.

Here comes the day!

The sun is rising! I send you my greeting!

You will recognize it by this sign: the dawn!

Ten times I greet you when the sun rises,

ten times when it shines,

and ten times too when it sets![46]

(38)

My love for her, I believe, forces me to wander
in a foreign country, all alone and poor.

I have no friend in whom I can confide in.
For company I have my camel mare and its saddle.

My love for her has made me forget
all those whom I have loved before.

She occupies a unique place
that no one else has occupied before her!

My passion for her dwells in my heart.
No other feeling, I know, can replace it.[47]

(39)

Poor crazy heart in its love for Leyla,

a child whose amulet has not yet been removed![48]

You must get cured.

Lovers always get cured.

The time has now come for you

to find a good doctor.

Why are you so inconsolable,

and if Leyla is so far away,

why do you feel as though

you are indebted to her

and must immediately pay her back your debt?

Is it reasonable

that neither all your misfortunes,

nor the anticipated and always postponed moment,

that nothing can make you forget her?[49]

(40)

Oh you crow,[50]

bird of absence,

your gloomy color

reminds me so well of the farewell's torments!

Let me know!

What do you say when you're resting?

Let me know!

What do you say when you're flying?

If your tales are true

then your sorrows are probably endless

and your wings are broken.

No one saves you

and you are always hunted,

like me, no one helps me

against those who oppress me.[51]

(41)

We had taken away the saddles
from our exhausted horses.
It was in Mecca.

I asked a mufti whom I met there:
"Tell me, by God, she whose memory
incessantly consumes my body,
will she be forgiven?

He answered: "Never.
Torments, by God, will fall upon her.
She will experience misery!"

I could not stop myself from breaking out into tears,
which ran down on my shirt's collar.
"O! May God forgive her her sins," I said.
"Forget, Oh God, that in this world she gave so little!"[52]

(42)

When Majnūn was in al-Khayf, he heard someone call the name "Leyla", which made him faint. His family gathered around him and his father cried of sorrow. When he woke up, he recited these verses.

We were in Minā,[53] in al-Khayf.[54]

A man shouted out a name,

reviving my soul's torments

without knowing it.

This call, it was Leyla's name...

- without Leyla -,

and I felt as though a bird flew out from my heart.

Someone called: "Leyla"

Oh, May God tire out his eyes!

As Leyla is in Damascus,

in the desert, in which places?

I tell my heart to be patient,

and it says:

"Be worried from this day,

but you must endure!

When your beloved is far away,

deported and fleeing,

your passion for her

burns more than glowing coal!"[55]

(43)

I did not beg during this pilgrimage
to make amends for a sin that I have committed,
but to receive assistance in renewing an old tie.

You have made me love her already as a young man
and you have made me fall madly in love with her.

Today I have become older.
So give me through her my reason back
or do so that the love between me and her
becomes mutual;

for You are know to be Just,
O my Merciful Lord,
in all Your deeds.[56]

(44)

During the pilgrim's days, Majnūn's father led him to a
gathering of people and begged them to pray for him. When they
started to pray, Majnūn recited these verses.

The pilgrims gather around me.

In Mecca one only heart pounds.

In this noise, among all these people,

my glowing thoughts go to you.

I have said in this holy place

in which our souls are pure and devoted to God:

"I am coming here, my Lord,

regretful and repenting all my sins,

Alas! All very obvious.

But about my love for Leyla,

if it is necessary that I do not visit her any more,

I cannot promise You that.

How can I do this?

My heart is her pledge.

To obey You or to be punished?

To abandon her for You? [57]

(45)

When Majnūn entered Mecca, he started asking God about Leyla. So his friends told him: "Isn't it better that you beg God to make you free from her and that you pray that He forgives you your sins?" He then recited these verses.

In this place in which the beasts are safe,[58]

and in which all the people,

- united horizons -,

become one.

By al-Ḥaṭīm[59] I have thought of you so much

that I felt that my soul was carrying its sorrow to you.

In Mecca, the pilgrim with uncombed hair,

is praying to God for His Mercy,

so that Leyla's sins become forgiven.

I have called: "O Merciful,

listen to me! First You must give me Leyla,

and then You can judge her!

If I have Leyla in this life,

then there will not be any man

who will repent for his sin

unless that with him

I shall repent for the same sin."

When she is close to me

she is the apple of my eye,

I love her even more

when she is criticized.

They tell me again and again:

"Think of God!", but I refuse

because I swear she is a need

that I will not repent for.

My soul has never hated you

to ever want to abandon you, Oh Leyla,

you who have given me so little happiness!

Come, be patient, Oh my heart!

You know it well:

you are not the first one

who has been separated from its beloved![60]

(46)

O Naᶜmān's[61] two mountains,

by God you must allow

this wind to send its breeze to me!

May my heart be consoled

and its sickness cured

by a fresh breath

that can revive me!

The one who inhales

the soft eastern wind

can appease the torments

in his anguished soul.

Naᶜmān, during long days,

has welcomed our tribes.

We embellished these places

when we pitched our camps there!

Oh wind, blow,

pass by the camp and tell me

whether its traces are still visible

or whether they are erased.

The sickness which has afflicted me,

Oh Leyla, is so old!

But if love's torments have lasted so long

they can only be more devastating!

I remember well our meetings in the mornings

when a white camel mare carried me forth to you.

Oh! How beautiful life was then,

happiness did not know any sorrow!

The reason why these tears are weakening my sight,

it is Leyla.

It is for her that one sees them pouring so,

and the wound in my eyes that never heals.

Oh my friends, dress this bleeding heart,

which soon shall be reduced into ashes![62]

(47)

When shall my tormented heart
ever be healed from you?

Death stretches its arrow,
it is hurrying.
It will reach me before I see you again.

Separation, love, longing, despair!
Neither you come to me
and nor I go to you.

My destiny is like the destiny of a bird
in a little girl's hand:
she presses it hard
and makes it taste of the cup of death.

But the girl is playing
and does not care for her victim:

she is too young to pity it,

and the bird is too weak to fly away.

Of course that I know about thousands of places

to where I can lead my steps,

but where shall I go to, my heart,

if you are not with me?[63]

(48)

Abandon me to my crazy wandering!
Don't you see that this weakened body
is going to its death?

My poor heart!
It has endured too much in this earth:
passion's glow, defeat and torments!

God's big country has become too little for me:
Oh my friends, who shall ever find
for the confused man a secure place in this world?

Our separation pains me,
the longing tortures me:
they are so far away the places where she lives
and our reunion has now become impossible!

Where is the road that leads to Leyla?

Are they hiding her for me now,

- me who have never encountered

an obstacle on this path before? -[64]

(49)

What slanders are poisoning Leyla's soul?
Is she thinking of me?
I forgive her her injustice.

Never has my heart hated you
to want to abandon you, Oh Leyla,
you who have given me so little happiness!

Oh how many times do the kindest persons
exclaim when they see me coming:
"Here comes Leyla's worshiper!"

When she is close to me
she is the apple of my eye.
I love her even more
when she is criticized.

They tell me again and again:

"Think of God", but I refuse,

for I swear she is a need

that I will not repent for![65]

(50)

Oh you who have forced me
to take a journey in the night,
at the time when the grey partridge
sleeps over Jilhatān.[66]

You who have angrily broken my heart.
You for whom I have cried rivers!

You who have turned all my people against me,
all of them indignant, furious,
driving me away with their resentment!

You who have not kept your promises.
You who have turned me
into a laughing-stock and into a scapegoat
before all those who yesterday were slandering you!

You who have pointed at me

and threw me as a victim,

all alone before the slanderers' words

without paying for your crimes!

Oh! If the slanders could mark a body,

I would fear very much

that on my body one could read all these words![67]

(51)

His family reproached him of loving Leyla. He then recited this poem to them. According to the tradition, it is indicated as the one that gave him the name Majnūn "the Madman".

Contemplate, Oh poor madman,

this heart snatched away

by an impossible love,

which you never can appease.

The love and longing that I have for her

have a hold on my heart and dwell within it.

Blessed is the man in this earth who shares your life!

God has spared him from torments and worries,

while for me, before each of the letters that you have sent me,

can only burst into tears at each of their words.

I encourage my heart to flee her,

it accepts.

But as soon that I say "It is best so",

my longing for her only increases.

I cannot stop myself

from loving this woman

and the love in my heart

can only intensify its torments.

Many times I could have followed

those you despise,

but my heart intoxicated by you

would not have obeyed.

Passion intensifies the more it is curbed:

Man loves nothing more than the forbidden fruit!

May they send my greetings to Leyla,

it is necessary that they do it now.

Death is on its way.

Am I dead or alive in this earth?

It is too unbearable for this impatient heart

which beats loud and cries![68]

(52)

I long for the earth of Al-Ḥidjāz,[69]

I need to see a camp in Najd.

But it is far away,

too far away,

it is invisible,

and it is of no use to look this way at Najd.

Is it good? Is it bad?

Continue! It is enough! It is too late.

I shall stay here and watch.

And in this manner! Day after day,

one look, one tear, one look.

Oh this water that fills my eyes and pours down!

When will peace come to my pounding heart?

It is either unhappy when she is near

or filled with longing when she is far.

They say: "See him crying.
She has destroyed him completely
and his tears keep on flowing."

But no, these are not tears
that are pouring down from my eyes,
but a soul that is gradually dripping.[70]

(53)

My bones have not longer any skin,
you have undressed them
and left then naked in the sunlight
and in the cold night.

See, they are emptied from their marrow
and remind of some hollow reed pipes
through which the wind sighs.

One day you will hear it,
and then, terrified, you will remember
the one who loves you.

The fear in your confused soul
will break down all the inhibitions.

Take my hand, lift me up
and see carefully all that you have caused.

But no, I shall hide it.

I am now destitute.

All of this is of no use

if you do not feel any compassion,

and if I do not find enough strength to abandon you.

I have done everything in my power, Oh God,

to make her happy,

and I am not anything else

but a loving man,

who is unfaithful to You.

No, these are not tears

that are pouring down from my eyes,

but a soul that is gradually dripping![71]

(54)

I looked at the camp
and I thought that I was seeing it behind a glass pane.

Love was rendering everything blurry,
and my eyes were drowning in tears
which were blinding me.

Other times, the water would withdraw,
and again I could see.

No, these are not tears
that are pouring down from my eyes,
but a soul that is gradually dripping![72]

(55)

I shall not go farther away, Oh Leyla,

twenty years, this is a too long time.

I shall wait for you here,

crying over my misery.

My love for you

is my sick heart's slayer,

but against the enemy,

if this one is loved,

what can one do?

I go where Leyla goes

and then she leaves me.

This is life:

people reunite and separate.

I think I have put around my heart a leash:

Leyla drags me and after her I follow.

Darkness surrounds my path

and I am shaking,

as though I were mad

and my members were dislocating.[73]

(56)

I am surprised that Leyla can fall asleep

when sleep cannot find its way any more to me.

When once, in spite of the separation's torments,

my eyes became heavy with sleep,

the beloved Leyla visited me.

- Oh she was so beautiful

that I almost died when I awoke! -

Leyla's spirit came to me

after having abandoned me

and silenced the complains

that have embittered me.[74]

(57)

When Leyla's husband and her father had traveled one day to Mecca, she sent her maid to Majnūn to give him the message that he was invited to visit her one night. He stayed with her until the morning and she said to him before he left: "Come to me every night as long as the people are away," which he did. The last night, he recited these verses.

Leyla is now mine,

as I only can meet her sometimes.

I cannot visit Leyla

after that her people return.

I love Leyla!

Truly, she is the biggest passion

that Destiny threatens to take away from me

with every day that passes.

Alas! I must now be separated from Leyla!

The caravan has arrived.

I can never delight in Leyla's love

after that her people have returned.[75]

(58)

I remember, Oh Leyla,

the years that passed

and all these days!

Oh continuous bliss,

Oh light-heartedness!

Oh days you passed in a flash

like the shadow of the lance,

and faster did your shadow disappear with Leyla!

You were happiness...

I was not happy.

I remember! Thamdīn:

we saw a fire glow,

it was Leyla!

Our horses, urged by my companions,

galloped quickly towards al-Ghaḍā.

One of us with falcon sight said:

"I see a star,

there alone, toward Yemen,

in the heart of the night!".

And I said: "No, it is Leyla,

this fire glowing high in the sky,

and it is for me that it has revealed itself."

Was it necessary, Oh my friends,

to ride through al-Ghaḍā?

Why did we hurry there?

If only these places had taken us

away with them in the night!

In me, Oh Leyla,

so many desires and worries have multiplied.

If the night leads me to you,

where are you?

The day that you tire of crying over me, Oh friends,

I shall find someone else who will cry.

His tears will pour

when I shall be unable more to cry.

I have experienced passion

already as a young man,

and if I am now writing poems

it is only to calm my despair.

Sometimes God unites the tormented lovers

who never believed more that they would unite.

Damn them, Oh God, all those who say:

"Life has done its work

and cured your love.

They are long time ago these days

when Leyla, clothed in linen,

brought back the cattle

home in the evenings!"

But her children

and children's children can grow up

everything that is hers

has a place like her in my heart.

If we sat alone

in a beautiful secluded place to talk,

we became exposed.

These places now horrify me!

May God shower Leyla and her girlfriends

with His good deeds

when they pitch their camps

in remote valleys!

Whether I am rich or poor

I can never forget her,

and when at night, a long road takes me

to my lover's arms

I do not regret anything!

Oh women, it is of no use

to put on make-up

on someone among you who is beautiful

with nice curves,

and then show her to me and say:

"This is Leyla!"

Alas my friends! I must endure, poor me,

the destiny that has fallen upon us both.

God gives her to another man and breaks my heart:

could he not have destroyed me in another way?

You have said: "Leyla has pitched her tent in Taymāʾ.[76]

All of the summer she will be there."

But I have seen the months of the summer flee.

Oh! Why is there such a long road, Oh Leyla,

that carries you away and separates you from me?

Suppose that I live up there,[77] in Ḥaḍramawt,[78]

and then a slanderer comes to Yamāma,

he will surely find his way to me!

But why do they all rejoice,
Oh! May God damn them, to know
that the ties between Leyla and me are now broken?
- I who have always wanted to control this love,
that at the end, when so much was taken away from me,
I found my master. -

Oh! May the love between her and me
become mutual,
may it remain strong
and never cause my defeat or success!

May the star rise and show me the way,
may the morning come and awake my longing.

A whole mile can separate me from Damascus:
if Canopus[79] appears to Damascus's people,
it is she whom I see.

When one talks in my presence of another Leyla,

the tears immediately start to wet my garments;

and if the southern wind blows toward her country,

I find myself in the night falling in love with the wind!

Are they forbidding me to meet Leyla?

Are they watching over her dwelling?

They cannot take away the verses from me!

I admit before God that I love you, Oh Leyla:

You rule my heart, but what am I to you?

God chooses: he smiles to another

and gives you to him.

God decides: he gives me love's longing

and despair.

I have dreamt too long of happy days,

O Umm Mālik:

my hair has become grey

and my reason has weakened.

Night after night, and I am counting the nights,

- I who have lived a life before,

without counting them! -

I leave the camp here.

I have the ability,

when I am alone in the night

and thinking of you

to see you!

You draw my looks to you even during the prayer,

but I must learn to look forward and not backward![80]

I am not an unbeliever,

but my passion for you

awakes my sorrow

and renders a doctor helpless.

A name, for me, is loveable

if it goes well with yours or resembles it.

She is my most beautiful dream, Oh friends,
or the longing that destroys!
The one who sides with me sides with her,
the one who sides with her sides with me.

Oh al-ᶜAqīq's[81] pigeon,
how many tears do I owe you!
You know it well,
these eyes are only crying for you.

What can I expect from life, my friends,
when I see my happiness put up for auction
and being bought by someone else?

Leyla treats me badly,
and then she says: "He is forgetting me."
But everyone knows in which state I am!

Among friends and lovers,
we are the ideal couple:
one soul in two bodies,

in spite of all our enemies.

We are two friends

with no hope of reuniting;

the only ones in the world?

No. But let them show us two friends

who decline from uniting!

It is true that I fear you,

I fear of seeing you again,

I fear even that life fulfills this desire.

I fear almost to see you in my dreams!

I hear them saying:

"Majnūn from the tribe of ᶜĀmir

needs only to take a rest."

And I answer: "How can I do that?

I am suffering,

I am mad of passion,

I am desperate.

Do not come close to me

so that you will not be contaminated!"

Oh Umm Mālik, the time will pass like that,

and then the fatal moment will arrive.

Destiny will carry my name:

everything will be said.

Oh the happiness of my eyes

when they lose themselves in your eyes,

ruled by a burning heart,

drowning in tears and clear!

It is you who decide

if you want to make my life a hell,

it is you who decide

if you want to make me happy.

Because of you,

I am now a poor shadow of myself,

cried over by all,

regardless of whether they hate or love me.

Shall they hit and punish Leyla

every time that I visit her,

and when she sees me, be angry at her

and even accuse her of committing a sin?

Every time that I start a journey on this earth,

I caress my camel mare

and lead her to where my heart inclines.

Toward the East and South

if Leyla calls me,

but even stronger, if Leyla waits for me,

is the longing to the North

that almost pulls me out of the saddle!

I want, I want to sleep,

but sleep refuses to come to me:

perhaps that your ghost will soon appear?

She is a sorceress; Alas! But even witchcraft

can sometimes be defeated by other powers

unless when it concerns me,

whom Leyla always holds in her spell.

When we are getting nearer to you

as the night surprises us,

our mounts are only led by my thoughts of you.

Ruled by the flames of desire

my heart releases the rein.

Oh consuming glow, Oh burning heart!

Take a rest by us, Oh Yemenite riders,

for our love is passing the night in Yemen.

Tell me when we have gone away,

did the creek of Naᶜmān continue to flow,

and did the valley continue to lead forth its streams to us

like in an act of love?

Oh Naᶜmān's pigeons, what a storm in my heart

you have awaken when you sang for me!

When one is alone,

one's tears do not harm one's honor,

but see, I have cried in front of my followers.

Oh pigeons, sing,

exchange your answers,

coo melodies,

rock my despair,

and may your songs predict a happy meeting

in the camp of al-Ghaḍā.

Follow me!

How shall I know, Oh Leyla,

if I ever will know it one day,

among all these white hairs that cover my head,

which are my part, your part or love's part?

The slanderers are saying evil things about you,

but do they know to whom

and about whom they are talking like this?

'

They say that the lovers, Oh Umm Mālik, disappear,

but the passion in my heart for ever glows.

,

I beg of you, my God,

if you have made Leyla to be my destiny,

then make her see me with the same loving eyes

that I am seeing her with!

Or else, free me from this passion,

as meeting her has been meeting my misfortune.

Oh! For a woman like Leyla

any man would want to kill himself,

even if like me,

he can accustom himself to despair.

If they forbid me to meet her,

then you could, Oh my friends,

prepare for me the bed of death and the shroud,

and pray to God that He has Mercy on me![82]

(59)

Sleep left me

and opened the way for new torments,

and love weakened my body's movements.

I looked at the Little Bear and the Pleiades.

Love is like this,

the smallest things become a burden through it.

This beautiful woman with the rosy cheeks

whom I have fallen in love with,

I see her in front of me,

a glowing and clear star,

rising in the sky.

I love you,

I am madly in love with you,

I am thinking of you only.

It is for you that my eyes are crying rivers.

I would have wanted,

I would have wanted

that your death were my death,

and that one only grave

held both our bodies![83]

(60)

Oh Leyla's grave,

if the women of Arabia and Persia saw you now

they would yell out mourning screams!

Oh Leyla's grave,

protect always in honor

the one who brought grace into our life!

Oh Leyla's grave,

she is now a stranger,

there is no uncle or cousin

who is standing by her side!

Never before, Oh grave,

you have embraced

such a noble and pure woman as Leyla!

Oh Leyla's grave,

they are far away today,

her mother, her aunt

and all those who have protected her life![84]

(61)

If beyond death

one asked the lovers:

"Oh lovers, have you become relieved

of your torments?"

They will answer honestly:

"It is true that our bodies

have turned into ashes,

but the fire of love

still burns in our hearts.

Our body's eyes,

when they want to express our sorrow,

have tears that have dried up in their corners,

but our soul's eyes, they,

have tears that incessantly flow!"[85]

(62)

I wish we were

two deer grazing in distant valleys,

in green fields where the *Hawzān*-herbs[86] grow.

I wish we were two doves in the desert,

flying to our nest in the evening.

I wish we were two sharks in the streams,

rocked in the evening by the big sea.

I dream, I see us:

my life, your life, together!

I see, I dream, and even death unites us,

in the grave's bed, side by side, together!

A resting place far away from the world,

Oh well-concealed grave!

There we will rise

to experience the resurrection's day,

the new life and the eternal union![87]

Notes to the Preface and Introduction

[1] Cf. *Arabic Morphology and Phonology* (23) and (328).

[2] *Majnun Leyla.*

[3] Another well-known poet of platonic poems is Jamīl b. Maᶜmar (d. 701). a poet of Medina, whose love for his cousin Buthayna reminds of Majnūn's love to Leyla. He writes for instance:
   "My friend, in your whole life,
   have you ever seen
   a slain man,
   weeping of love for his slayer?" (Cf. *Mufīd* I, 213).

[4] One of the most famous poets of erotic poetry is ᶜUmar b. Al-Rabīᶜa (d. 712/744) who courted many beautiful women on their pilgrim journeys to Mecca and Medina (cf. *Encyclopédie de l'Amour* 323.)

[5] His whole name is Qays b. al-Mulawwaḥ. Muzāḥim b. ᶜUds b. Rabīᶜa b. Jaᶜda b. Kaᶜb b. ᶜĀmir b. Ṣaᶜṣaᶜ.

[6] *Aghānī* II, 1-78.

[7] Cf. *Dīwān* 20-21, *Aghānī* 2, 6 and *ᶜAynī* 1, 374.

[8] For a discussion of a few women see *Dīwān* 28-29.

[9] Cf. *Diwān* 21, *Aghānī* 2, 8 and *ᶜAynī* 1, 375.

[10] Her whole name is Leylā bint Mahdīy b. Saᶜd b. Mahdiyy b. Rabīᶜa b. al-Ḥuraysh b. Kaᶜb b. Rabīᶜa b. Saᶜṣaᶜa.

[11] Cf. *Dīwān* 10-11.

[12] Cf. ibid 11.

[13] Cf. ibid 15.

[14] Cf. ibid 299 and the notes, *Aghānī* II, 24, *Basṭ* 80 and *Tazyīn* 64.

[15] Cf. *Dīwān* 15.

[16] Cf. ibid 23-24.

[17] Cf. ibid 25, *al-Mustaṭraf* II, 194.

[18] Cf. *Layli and Majnun.*

[19] *Essential Rumi*, 6.

Notes to the Poems

¹ Metre *wāfir*. The rhyme is *-āʾu*. See *Dīwān* nr. 2 and *Zahra* 329.

² Al-Batīl is a mountain in Najd.

³ Metre *ṭawīl*. The rhyme is *-aṣdi*. See *Dīwān* nr. 94, *Basṭ* 75, *Aghānī* II, 23 and *Maṣāriᶜ* 271.

⁴ Metre *ṭawīl*. The rhyme is *-mu (-amu* or *-umu)*. See *Dīwān* nr. 238 and *Basṭ* 94.

⁵ Metre *ṭawīl*. The rhyme is *-ādiyā*. See *Dīwān* nr. 315.

⁶ Metre *ṭawīl*. The rhyme is *-iyā*. See ibid nr. 314 and *Zahra* 349.

⁷ The rhyme is *-aᶜu*. See *Dīwān* nr. 176.

⁸ Metre *ṭawīl*. The rhyme is *-tu (-ītu* or *-ūtu)*. See ibid nr. 58, *Basṭ* 80 and *Zahra* 208.

[9] The rhyme is -*šmi*. See *Dīwān* nr. 258 and *Basṭ* 93.

[10] The rhyme is -*aqu*. See *Dīwān* nr. 197 and *Basṭ* 80.

[11] Metre *ṭawīl*. The rhyme is -*ūdihā*. See *Dīwān* nr. 88 and *Basṭ* 89.

[12] The rhyme is -*li*. See *Dīwān* nr. 224.

[13] The rhyme is -*ri*. See ibid nr. 149.

[14] Metre *ṭawīl*. The rhyme is -*ašri*. See ibid nr. 143.

[15] Metre *ṭawīl*. The rhyme is -*&bi*. See ibid nr. 47.

[16] Metre *ṭawīl*. The rhyme is -*āni*. See ibid nr. 283.

[17] Metre *ṭawīl*. The rhyme is -*āʾibu*. See ibid nr. 5 and *Basṭ* 89.

[18] Metre *wāfir*. The rhyme is -*ārā*. See *Dīwān* nr. 155.

The house symbolizes the tent and the walls the tent's gore.

[19] Metre *wāfir*. The rhyme is -*ābā*. See ibid nr. 54.

[20] Metre *ṭawīl*. The rhyme is -*ībuhā*. See ibid nr. 40 and *Basṭ* 94.

[21] See *Dīwān* nr. 41.

[22] See ibid nr. 239. The rhyme is -*amu*.

[23] Metre *ṭawīl*. The rhyme is -*ībuhā*. See ibid nr. 38, *Basṭ* 93 and *Zahra* 120.

[24] Metre *ṭawīl*. The rhyme is *-buhā (-ibuhā* or *-ubuhā*. See *Dīwān* nr. 39 and *Zahra* 120.

The last verses are understood as though Majnūn has identified himself with the wolf and does not want to live any more if he cannot continue to wander around the camp.

[25] Metre *ṭawīl*. The rhyme is *-buhā   (-ībuhā* or *-ūbuhā).* See *Dīwān* nr. 37 and *Masālik* IX, 140.

[26] Metre *ṭawīl*. The rhyme is *-qu (-īqu* or *-ūqu).* See *Dīwān* nr. 199, *Tazyīn* 62 and *Amālī* I, 197.

[27] Metre *ṭawīl*. The rhyme is *-ṣdu.* See *Dīwān* nr. 74, *Aghānī* II, 65, and *Zahra* 220.

[28] Al-ᶜĀmirīya indicates that Leyla pertains to the Banū ᶜĀmir tribe.

[29] Metre *wāfir*. The rhyme is *-āḥu.* See *Dīwān* nr. 64, *Basṭ* 89, *Aghānī* II, 48, 62, 89, 92 and *Zahra* 159-160.

[30] One can compare the theme of the kiss with the one in Baudelaire's poem *Le Vampire* in *Les Fleurs du Mal:*

> "Tes baisers ressusciteraient
> Le cadavre de ton vampire ."
> ("*Your kiss would soon resuscitate*
> *The cold cadaver of your vampire.*") See *The Flowers of Evil.*

[31] Metre *ṭawīl*. The rhyme is *-ītu.* See *Dīwān* nr. 59.

[32] Metre *ṭawīl*. The rhyme is *ā§idi*. See ibid nr. 90 and *Zahra* 439.

[33] The word that the poet uses to refer to the earth's heightening is *mankib* "shoulder", which is a metaphor for "hill".

[34] The poet refers to *ṣadā*, which according to the pre-Islamic beliefs refers to an invisible bird that holds the dead person's soul and flies over his/her grave, cf. *Arabic-English Lexicon* II, 1670-1671.

[35] I am reminded of the verses written by the Swedish poet Esaias Tegnér (1782-1846) in his poem "Den döde" *(The Dead one")*, see *Dikt* p. 284:

> "ty döden själv kan ej min kärlek hämma
> och var jag är förnimmer jag din stämma"
> (*"As death itself cannot curb my love,
> And wherever I am I can hear your voice"*).

[36] Metre *ṭawīl*. The rhyme is *-bu (-abu, -ibu* or *-ubu)*. See *Dīwān* nr. 7, *Aghānī* II, 55 and *Zahra* 333.

[37] Metre *ṭawīl*. The rhyme is *-muhā*. See *Dīwān* nr. 254.

[38] Thabīr is a famous mountain in Mekka.

[39] Metre *ṭawīl*. The rhyme is *-bu (-abu* or *-ibu)*. See *Dīwān* nr. 8, *Aghānī* II, 55 and *Zahra* 333.

[40] "The damned", literally *ahl al-nār* "the people of hell".

[41] Metre *wāfir*. The rhyme is *-ūdu*. See *Dīwān* nr. 83.

[42] Metre *ṭawīl*. The rhyme is *-iruh*. See ibid nr. 127.

[43] Metre *ṭawīl*. The rhyme is *-ābi*. See ibid nr. 43 and *Basṭ* 90.

[44] The tradition describes Majnūn "the madman" as playing with stones and drawing in the sand.

[45] Metre *ṭawīl*. The rhyme is *-u (-aʾu* or *-uʾu)*. See *Dīwān* nr. 173 and *Basṭ* 89.

[46] Metre *ṭawīl*. The rhyme is *–ūᶜuhā*. See *Dīwān* nr. 183 and *Basṭ* 91.

[47] Metre *ṭawīl*. The rhyme is *-§lu*. See *Dīwān* nr. 208, *Aghānī* II, 46, *Tazyīn* 54 and *Basṭ* 72, 73.

[48] The amulet hangs around the child's neck in order to protect him/her against the evil eye.

[49] Metre *ṭawīl*. The rhyme is *-mah (-ā§imuh* or *ā§umuh)*. See *Dīwān* nr. 247, *Basṭ* 83 and *Aghānī* II, 6.

[50] The crow symbolizes the lovers' separation.

[51] Metre *ṭawīl*. The rhyme is *-īru*. See *Dīwān* nr. 124, *Basṭ* 84, *Amālī* I, 183, *Samt* 451 and *Zahra* 249.

[52] Metre *ṭawīl*. The rhyme is *-āluhā*. See *Dīwān* nr. 220, *Basṭ* 75, *Tazyīn* 66 and *Maṣāriᶜ* 270.

[53] Minā is one of Mecca's pilgrim places.

[54] Al-Khayf is the name of a mosque in Minā.

[55] Metre *ṭawīl*. The rhyme is *-§ri*. See *Dīwān* nr. 144, *Basṭ* 75, 85, *Zahra* 167-168 and *Masālik* IX, 142.

[56] Metre *ṭawīl.* The rhyme is *-aṣli.* See *Dīwān* nr. 227.

[57] Metre *wāfir.* The rhyme is *-bu (ibu* or *-ubu).* See ibid nr. 30.

[58] *Ḥaythu asta'mana l-waḥshu* "[in this place] where the beasts are safe," refers to the prohibition of killing animals in and around Kaᶜba in Mecca.

[59] Al-Ḥaṭīm is a place in Mekka.

[60] Metre *ṭawīl.* The rhyme is *-buhā (-ībuhā* or *-ūbuhā).* See *Dīwān* nr. 33, *Basṭ* 75, 92, *Samṭ* 900 and *Maṣāriᶜ* 251.

[61] Naᶜmān is a region that Leyla usually visits.

[62] Metre *ṭawīl.* The rhyme is *-muhā (-īmuhā* or *-ūmuhā).* See *Dīwān* nr. 251, *Aghānī* II, 26, *Tazyīn* 60 and *Zahra* 221, 231.

[63] Metre *ṭawīl.* The rhyme is *-abu.* See *Dīwān* nr. 6, *Basṭ* 89 and *Masālik* IX, 143.

[64] Metre *basīṭ.* The rhyme is *-bu (-abu, -ibu* or *-ubu).* See *Dīwān* nr. 11.

[65] Metre *ṭawīl.* The rhyme is *-buhā (-ībuhā* or *-ūbuhā).* See ibid nr. 34 and *Masālik* IX, 140.

[66] Jilhatān is a place which is hard to identify, cf. *Ṣifat jazīrat al-ᶜarab* 220.

[67] Metre *ṭawīl.* The rhyme is *-mu (-īmu* or *-ūmu).* See *Dīwān* nr. 246, *Aghānī* II, 59 and *Zahra* 42.

[68] Metre *basīṭ.* The rhyme is *-ᶜā.* See *Dīwān* nr. 191 and *Aghānī* II, 37.

[69] Al-Ḥidjāz is a mountainous province in the Arabian Peninsula that runs along the west-central coast. Najd is a region in central Saudi Arabia, comprising a rocky plateau sloping eastward from al-Ḥidjāz.

[70] Metre *ṭawīl*. The rhyme is *-ru (-aru, -iru* or *-uru)*. See *Dīwān* nr. 116 and *Zahra* 203.

[71] Metre *ṭawīl*. The rhyme is *-ru (-aru, -iru* or *–uru)*. See *Dīwān* nr. 117, *Tārīkh Baghdād* X, 211, *Tazyīn* 64 and *Amālī* I, 162.

[72] Metre *ṭawīl*. The rhyme is *-ru (-iru* or *-uru)*. See *Dīwān* nr. 118, *Zahra* 295, *Amālī* I, 208 and *Aghānī* XVII, 138.

[73] Metre *ṭawīl*. The rhyme is *ᶜu*. See *Dīwān* nr. 172.

[74] The rhyme is *-lu*. See ibid nr. 215.

[75] The rhyme is *–uhā*. See ibid nr. 249 and *Aghānī* II, 72.

[76] Taymāʾ is an oasis in North Arabia.

[77] Up there refers to the mountains of the country.

[78] Ḥaḍramawt is a province in South Arabia. These verses have been mentioned and translated in my book *Arabic Morphology* 102-103.

[79] "Canopus" *suhayl* shows the direction to the beloved or symbolizes her.

[80] Forward and not backward: it is understood here that Leyla is standing among the women behind the men during the prayer

and that Majnūn is looking backward at her instead of looking
forward as the others in the direction of Mecca.

[81]   Al-ᶜAqīq refers to a valley.

[82]   Metre *ṭawīl*. The rhyme is *-āṣiyā*. See *Dīwān* nr. 307, *Basṭ*
85-89, *Masālik* IX, 138, 143, 144, *Aghānī* I, 8, 417, II, 10, 34,
36, 40, 54, 68, 69, 70, 77, 78, 93, IV, 291, 292, *Zahra* 26, 28,
40, 260, 303, 332, *Maṣāriᶜ* 238, *Amālī* I, 215, 221 and *Khizāna*
IV, 295.

This poem is called *al-muᵓnisa* "the reliable one" and is the
longest in the collection.

[83]   Metre *wāfir*. The rhyme is *-&du (-īdu* or *-ūdu)*. See *Dīwān*
nr. 81.

[84]   Metre *ṭawīl*. The rhyme is *-am*. See ibid nr. 257 and *Maṣāriᶜ*
296-297.

[85]   Metre *basīṭ*. The rhyme is *-bu (-abu* or *-ibu)*. See *Dīwān* nr.
12.

[86]   *Ḥawzān* is a herb that grows in the plains and that tastes
good.

[87]   Metre *ṭawīl*. The rhyme is *-a&ri*. See *ibid* nr. 145.

Bibliography

Arabic-English Lexicon = *Arabic-English Lexicon*, Lane, 2 Band, Cambridge 1984.

Aghānī = *Al-Aghānī*, Maṭbaᶜat Dār al-Kutub wa-Būlāq.

Amālī = *Al-Amālī*, Dār al-Kutub.

Basṭ = *Basṭ sāmiᶜ al-masāmir*, nr 375 of the Taymūrīya collections *(majāmīᶜ taymūrīya)* in Dār al-Kutub.

Dikt = Svensk dikt från trollformler till Lars Norén, en antologi sammanställd av docent Lars Gustafsson, Stockholm 1978 - Great Brittain 1980.

Dīwān = *Dīwān majnūn Leylā*, ed. ᶜAbd al-Sattār Aḥmad Farrāj, Dār miṣr lil-ṭibāᶜā.

Encyclopédie de l'Amour = *Encyclopédie de l'Amour en Islam*, Malek Chebe, 2003.

Essential Rumi = *Essential Rumi*, translations by Coleman Barks with John Moyne, NY 1996.

Khizāna = *Khizānat al-adab li-l-Baghdādī*, Būlāq 1299.

Layli and Majnun: Love, Madness and Mystic Longing, Dr. Ali Asghar Seyed-Gohrab, Brill Studies in Middle Eastern literature, Jun 2003.

Les Fleurs du Mal = *Les Fleurs du Mal et autres poèmes,* Ch. Baudelaire, Paris 1964.

Majnūn, l'amour poème, choix de poèmes traduits de l'arabe et présentés par André Miquel, Paris 1984.

Majnun Leyla = *Majnun Leyla, Arabiska Kärleksdikter,* Åkesson, J., in: Alhambras Litterära magasin, pp. 47-49, 1994, nr 4.

Masālik = *Masālik al-abṣār,* a Manuscript in Dār al-Kutub.

Maṣāri[c] = *Maṣāri*[c] *al-*[c]*ushshāq,* Maṭba[c]at al-Jawā°ib 1301 A.H.

Mufīd = *al-Mufīd fī-l-adab al-*[c]*arabī,* J. Hāshim, A. Sa[c]d, A. Abu– Ḥāqa, I. Ḥāwī, Band I, Beirut 1984.

*Al-Mustaṭraf,*1292 A.H.

Samṭ = *Samṭ al-la°ālī,* Maṭba[c]at lajnat al-ta°līf.

Ṣifat jazīrat al-[c]*arab* = *Ṣifat jazīrat al-*[c]*arab,* Ḥamdāni, Ed. D. H. Müller, Leiden 1968.

Tārīkh Baghdād, Maṭba[c]at as-Sa[c]āda 1349 A.H.

Tazyīn = *Tazyīn al-aswāq,* al-Maṭba[c]a al-Azharīya 1328, 3rd edition.

The Flowers of Evil, William Aggeler, Guild, 1954.

The Story of Layla and Majnun by Nizami, trans. and ed. by Rudolf Gelpke in collaboration with E. Mattin and G. Hill, Omega Publications, New Lebanon, NY, 1997.

Zahra = *Az-Zahra,* Beirut 1351.